'Famil

Often desc
owners are
have an ab
more train
zest for life, they can have seemingly endless levels of energy. They can sometimes forget your existence when following a scent, or simply ignore you to play with other dogs.

Many of the Poo's I have worked with have been nervous or shy of people, a little 'flighty'. Some can be 'whiney' or 'barky' and jump up. All of this means that socialisation and training are key for these dogs to build confidence.

Crossed Wires

he 'Spaniel' in your cross was bred for gundog ork and this means the breed are often very scent riven. They require more mental stimulation and ental games than lots of other breeds. Many enjoy roblem solving or simply having something to do.

The 'Poodle' was originally bred for duck hunting and so water and retrieves can play a big part in this dogs' make up. The Miniature Poodle was used for scenting out truffles in the woods. They are well known for being good at scentwork. By combining these breeds we are not watering down each of the breeds, but more often gaining the characteristics of both breeds in one dog.

s the owner of a Cockapoo you are responsible for fulfilling his 'breed needs'. Vhilst each dog is an individual it is highly likely that he will want to use his ose and his brain. Tap into these breed drives and use them to your advantage. earn about your breed and provide a suitable outlet for behaviours which e highly likely to come out in his behaviour in some way or another. This ay mean you train each day, teach a retrieve, teach scent work, try gundog aining or agility. Whatever it is you do, you and your Poo will benefit from it!

TRICK TRAINING

You may think that tricks are either too difficult for you to train or that your dog has no real need for them. Think again!

What is a *sit* or a *down* if not a simple trick? Many tricks have practical uses, but key to training tricks is the bond you develop between you and your Poo and also the confidence which tricks allow your dog to feel. The more they know the more appropriate behaviours they have to use!

JO AND WICKET'S FAVOURITE TRICKS

Hand Touch (Target Training)

The hand touch is such a simple and fun trick to train. It is also very useful and can be used as an alternative to a recall cue, to keep your Poo amused at the vets and can be trained straight from your armchair!

What do you need?
- Rewards (tiny pieces of fresh chicken are my dog's favourite)
- Clicker (or marker word)
- You and your Poo!

How?
- With your clicker and rewards at the ready, hold your flat hand out to the side of your Poo's snout, quite close.
- As he turns his face to investigate your hand click and reward.
- Take your hand away and present it again. Click and reward as your Poo's nose touches your hand.
- Repeat several times until your Poo understands he is being clicked for touching your hand.
- If you can bet £50 that when you hold out your hand your Poo will touch it with his snout then you are ready to add your cue word.
- Say 'Touch' then hold out your hand to the side of your Poo's face. Click and treat when he touches your hand.
- Once he has it, you can start to be more adventurous and ask a little more of your Poo. Try the other hand or move your hand further away, and use your cue word 'Touch'.

Meerkat

Another favourite of mine and one your Poo should pick up quickly. A fun trick which makes your dog look cute and clever but also to build those core tummy muscles.

How?

- With your Poo in a sit, take a piece of food in your hand and hold your hand just in front of his nose.
- Slowly move your hand upwards and little back over your Poo's head so that his front paws leave the floor.
- Click and reward as your Poo's feet come off the floor.
- Some dogs can instantly raise their two paws off the floor others need to build up their strength to do this.

Always choose a trick which suits your dog's physical capabilities.

THE GREAT OUTDOORS

Socialisation
It's not a dirty word!

In my experience Cockapoos need as much, or even more socialisation than many other breeds.

Some can be on the shy side and need to get used to handling, the noise and bustle of family life and the great outdoors.

As a family dog your Poo needs to experience all it is going to face as an adult whist still young. This needs to be done repeatedly and with an understanding of your Poo's body language so that you don't terrify your new pup.

Cockapoo puppies need to see, hear and meet dogs of different breeds, people of all kinds, children of all ages and experience all of the environments they are going to have to visit when they are fully grown.

Sit on a park bench with your puppy and let the world go by whilst your puppy watches and absorbs from a safe distance. If you plan to take your Poo to the pub or coffee shop when he's older don't wait until he's older to do it – take him there now!

Signs your dog is uncomfortable or scared:
Tail tucked, ears pinned back, backing off from a person or child, hiding, shaking, barking to tell them to move away.

If your Poo puppy is showing any of these signs then you need to take things a little slower, build up their exposure slowly in a calm and kind way, rewarding his bravery with yummy food rewards. If needed call a trainer to help you with this.

The Great Escape

Recall training is a priority. The better your Poos recall the more fun you can have outdoors with him and also the healthier and happier your Poo will be.

In the big wide world you are competing with a very exciting environment to gain your Poo's attention. Many owners simply leave their dogs to it and chat with friends or on their mobile whilst their dog reinforces his own behaviour by doing absolutely anything and everything he wants. Quite simply he is ignoring you and really doesn't care whether or not you are on the walk.

I would rather be the 'bee's knees' to my Poo, I want him to see me as the person to run to for help when he needs it, to play with when he wants and to come to when I call.

Recall needs to be trained in a quiet environment at first, not too many distractions or other dogs, so that you are his focus. Do the following training at home in the living room, in the kitchen, in the garden, outside the house, then at the park in a quiet area. This way you set both you and your Poo up to succeed.

I believe the core of your recall is eye contact associated to your dog's name. If you haven't got a dog who looks at you when you say their name then you have very little to build on. So, train this first. Then use recall games to train your Poo to come to you whilst having fun!

Eye Contact:

What do you need?
- High value food rewards
- Clicker (or marker word)
- You and your Poo!

How?
- Say your Poo's name.
- The moment he looks at you click and reward him with a yummy treat.
- Repeat.
- You really need to pay attention, so watch your dog carefully, as he may only give you a flicker of attention and it is important to catch it when he does.

Once he is making eye contact with you whenever you say his name try this:

- Hold a piece of food out away from you at shoulder height.
- Say his name.
- Click when he turns away from the food you are holding and makes eye contact, reward with the food. You should see him clearly look from the food you are holding out to your face.
- Its not easy for a dog to look away from food!

Recall Circuits:

These circuits are a brilliant way to teach recall using a fun game.

What do you need?

Food rewards (quite big so they can be seen and a contrasting colour to the ground you are throwing them on e.g. chicken shows up well on grass)

Your and your Poo!

How?

With a treat in your hand and with your Poo's attention on you, throw the food a short distance so that your dog runs to get it.

Call your Poo back to you and with another treat ready in your hand, lure them around your body behind you and throw the food back out as a reward.

Call your Poo back to you and repeat the circuit.

Soon your Poo should be running back to you and around your body without the treat as a lure and you can simply reward them for this by throwing their treat out again.

Jo's Top Tip:

Call your Poo to you many times on a walk so that they don't associate you calling them with the fun being over and going home.

WHO'S WALKING WHO?

It's such a pleasure to be able to enjoy walking with your Poo on a loose lead. If you have a new puppy start as you mean to go on by never allowing your pup to pull you around. Dogs do what works, and if it works to pull you then they will repeat it! Who can blame them? – it's being reinforced after all. Instead, stand still when your dog pulls and train your dog to walk beside you with a loose lead with the method below.

If you have already got a 'puller' then follow the steps below to get your cockapoo walking nicely on the lead.

What do you need?
- Yummy high value food rewards
- A lead
- Clicker (or marker word if you prefer)
- Practice! This takes a little co-ordination but you'll get there!
- You and your Poo!

How?
- Start training indoors, in a calm environment. You do not need lots of space.
- Hold your lead and clicker in your right hand, placed at your belt buckle.
- Keep your food in your left hand, with your hand high up on your chest so that you are not luring your Poo with food.
- Stand still and wait for a loose lead, as soon as you get it, click and reward, placing the food at the back of your left heel.
- Don't be tempted to move yet – we want your Poo to learn that they are being rewarded for the lead being loose. If the dog pulls don't budge at all. Brace yourself. Wait for that lead to go loose again and click and reward at your left heel.
- Repeat.
- Now try taking a step. If the lead is still loose click and reward as above and take a few more steps.
- If your Poo pulls, stand still and wait for slack in the lead and click and reward placing the treat at the back of your left heel.
- Try to reward your dog before they get to the point of pulling you so that they learn the correct behaviour and are set up to succeed.

Jo's Top Tip:
Reward a LOT at first to really get this behaviour going.

BRILLIANTLY BRAINY BREED!

You shouldn't be shocked to hear that your Cockapoo is in fact made up of two different breeds, each of which comes with it's own inherent breed drives. These are natural behaviours, which rather than being punished should be provided with an acceptable outlet.

BRAIN GAMES

Use brain games to provide an outlet for your Poos breed instincts. This will keep your Poo happy and healthy and hopefully you too!

THE SHAPE GAME

Simply pick up your clicker and place a cardboard box (with all staples and Sellotape removed) in the middle of the room. Get ready to click for your Poo going over to investigate. Then reward with a yummy reward inside the box.

Now wait and click when your Poo returns to the box – maybe they put a paw inside this time, or perhaps they shove the box with their nose. Decide what it is you'd like your Poo to do and click and reward them for doing it.

So many behaviours can be clicked and rewarded by 'shaping' them in this way! A real game for the brain!

KING KONG

Stuff a Kong with yummy food mixed with your Poo's normal food and give it to him when you have things you need to do. This will keep him amused whilst you're on the phone or at your laptop. Use the Kong to entertain your Poo when guests arrive or simply to give him something to do! Remember a bored Poo finds his own entertainment – usually chewing the table legs or digging holes in the lawn!

Food ideas to stuff a Kong; cream cheese, frozen yoghurt, pate, dried kibble, marmite, dried dog biscuits

> **Jo's Top Tip:**
> **If your Poo finishes the Kong very quickly make it more difficult for him by freezing the Kong first!**

KEEPING AGILE

Create a simple agility course in your garden using towels for jumps, an old kids play tunnel, canes make good weave poles too! Or if budget allows find a simple set to buy. Practise the cues you have taught your dog whilst doing this; use sit stays and down stays, teach jump and weave etc

PASSION FOR PADDLING

Many Cockapoos love the water. Mine loves to run through the sprinkler in my garden on a hot day! Why not provide a paddling pool for your Poo to play in? A hard plastic one should prevent it getting popped. Remember supervision is needed for your dog and any children in the family.

If you find your Poo is a little unsure of the water perhaps throw a few favourite toys or a ball in and see if that encourages him. In winter months the water can be replaced with a ball pit or sand.

COMMON SCENTS

Dogs need to sniff and Cockapoos really enjoy doing it! Use up that extra energy by providing scent games for your Poo.

TRY A TRAIL

With your Poo either being held on lead or in a sit-stay, take one of his toys and walk through grass ensuring you leave an obvious scent trail as you walk. Place your Poo's toy on the floor at the end of the scent trail. Return to your Poo and let him lead you to the toy.

DROP YOUR GLOVES

Simply drop one of your gloves as you walk and walk past the glove for a few steps. Stop and make a noise to indicate you've lost your glove and then go back, with your Poo and point out the glove and reward your dog for 'finding' the glove with you. Within a few trials your Poo should have caught on to the game and should be looking for the glove themselves. Reward this and then start to make the game a little harder by dropping the glove and walking a little further away.

LOST AND FOUND

Hide treats around the house or garden and let your Poo find them. Help him at first by leading him around the trail you have laid to make sure he understands. With practise you will be able to send him to find the trail. Once your Poo has caught on use the cue 'find it' to send him to look for the food trail.

COAT MANAGEMENT

Managing a Cockapoo coat can be tricky. It is really important to do this when they are a puppy to ensure you don't have problems later. Your groomer will be hugely grateful, I assure you!

TO SHED OR NOT TO SHED?

Coats vary from one Poo to the next. Some can take on the Poodle coat, some the Spaniel coat and any combination in between. Your dog may have a very different puppy coat to its adult coat. Whatever the coat it is highly likely to need regular grooming. My Poo visits the groomers roughly every 7 weeks to keep his coat in good shape and I groom key areas, such as the ears and tail and under his arms, each morning to keep them tangle free. Some Cockapoos are prone to matting so manage this by regularly grooming these key areas. Managing a Cockapoo coat takes time, probably more time than hoovering up dog hair from a shedding dog. Also, some Poos shed and some don't, you never quite know what you're gonna get!

HANDLING YOUR POO

Most Poo's enjoy being fussed or stroked but when it comes to touching their paws, clipping their nails, cleaning their ears or simply drying their wet feet when they come in from the garden, they really don't enjoy it. Often these key requirements of Cockapoo ownership are left. Get your Poo used to this kind of handling using the following method.

TOUCH AND TREAT

Choose a time of day when you can sit down quietly with your calm (ish!) puppy and touch your puppy and then reward this with a treat. Simply touch a paw gently and reward with food. If your Poo mouths your hands they are telling you they are not comfortable with what you are doing and are trying to let you know to stop. Take things slowly and reward each touch. Build up to touching puppy with a brush and gentle strokes, rewarding as you go. Many Poos really struggle with this so take things slowly and put the effort in to get the results you want.

> **Jo's Top Tip:**
> If your Poo really struggles with the touch and treat approach;
> Use a stuffed Kong and whilst he is eating brush him gently,
> stopping when he stops eating and starting again when he
> returns to eating from the Kong. It's two-way communication.

Find a good groomer to take your Poo to for mini sessions to get him used to the environment, noise, dryers, other dogs, getting nails clipped etc. Build up to a full cut so you don't overwhelm your pup. Ensure your groomer uses positive reinforcement methods and has a good understanding of dog body language so they can tell when your Poo is uncomfortable and take things at your Poo's pace.

IS YOUR POO A SOCK THIEF?

My own Poo loves to steal socks and other unmentionables from the laundry basket. I have seen him stealing them from the washing machine or tumble dryer too. Why not turn it into a really cool trick where your dog can help put washing in and out of the washing machine? Many assistance dogs learn these 'tricks'.

Why do our Poo's 'steal'?

Often this behaviour starts as a fun attention seeking or exploration game, socks are just soft toy like things to them after all – many of us react to this cheeky behaviour and the most amazing game of chase, to get the stolen item back, occurs. In my experience many Poo's have a tendency to show this kind of behaviour, perhaps due to their gundog traits, and preventing it is much better than curing it.

This behaviour can transfer to other objects which our dogs see as valuable. What kind of a reaction does your Poo get when he 'steals' Gran's glasses or the TV remote?